# The Earth

by Carol Levine

# The Earth's Natural Resources

Our planet is rich in many ways. We use these riches every day. Scientists call these riches **natural resources.** A natural resource is a useful thing that comes from nature.

Some natural resources, such as oil and coal, can be used up. Other natural resources, such as trees, can be replaced when they are used. Some natural resources cannot be used up. Sunlight and air cannot be used up.

# Water and Air

Living things need water. There is fresh water on Earth. It is found in ponds, rivers, and lakes. There is also salt water. It is found in oceans and seas.

Plants, animals, and people use water in many ways. Think of all the ways you use water.

Living things need air too. Air is all around us. Wind is moving air. We cannot see air, even when it moves.

Animals and plants need air to live. People need air to breathe.

Water and air are natural resources.

# Rocks and Soil

Rocks are a natural resource. Rocks can be different sizes. Rocks can be different shapes and colors too.

People use rocks for many things. We use them to make roads and buildings.

Large rocks are called
**boulders.** Rocks are broken
down by wind, rain, and ice.
**Sand** is made up of many
small rocks.

gold

Gold and garnets are
used to make jewelry.

garnet

Rocks are made of **minerals.** Minerals are nonliving things. They are natural resources. People use minerals all the time. Gold, silver, and iron are some minerals we use.

iron

Iron is used to make bridges.

Soil covers most of the land on Earth. This natural resource is made of many parts. Clay, sand, humus, air, and water are in soil. Soil is a mixture of these parts.

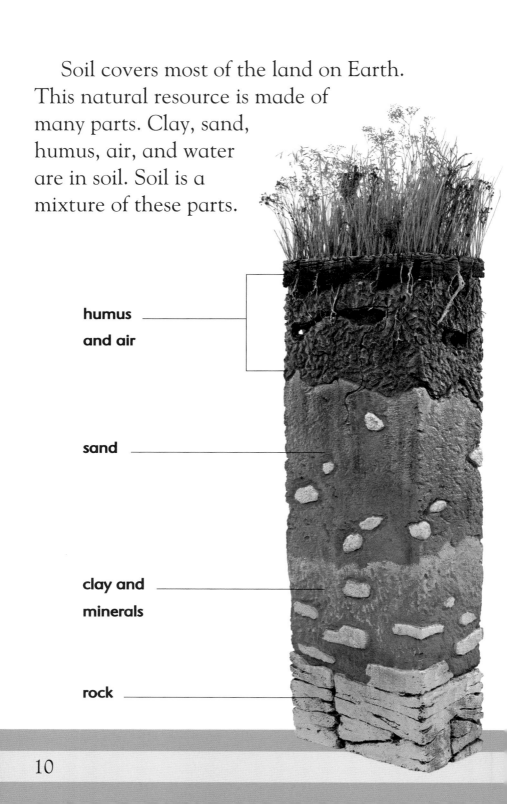

humus
and air

sand

clay and
minerals

rock

There are different kinds of soil. Soil can be different colors. Soil can feel hard, crumbly, or soft. Soil can be wet or dry. Different plants grow in different soil. Some plants like salty soil. Potatoes grow best in loose, sandy soil.

# Plants

Plants are a natural resource. Plants have different parts. People use parts of plants in many ways. We use wood from trees to build houses. We use lots of plants as food.

small sugar pumpkins 59¢/lb.

# Erosion And Weathering

Earth changes all the time. Erosion and weathering change the Earth. **Erosion** is when water or wind moves the rocks or soil. Plants help stop erosion. Their roots hold on to the soil.

Weathering also changes the Earth. **Weathering** is when ice, wind, and rain break and change rocks. Weathering happens slowly.

# Pollution

People can change the Earth. Some changes can harm the planet. The Earth is harmed when bad things are put into the land, air, or water. This is called **pollution.** Pollution is dangerous for plants, animals, and people.

People can help make less pollution. Trash is a big part of pollution. When people pick up their trash, they are helping to stop pollution.

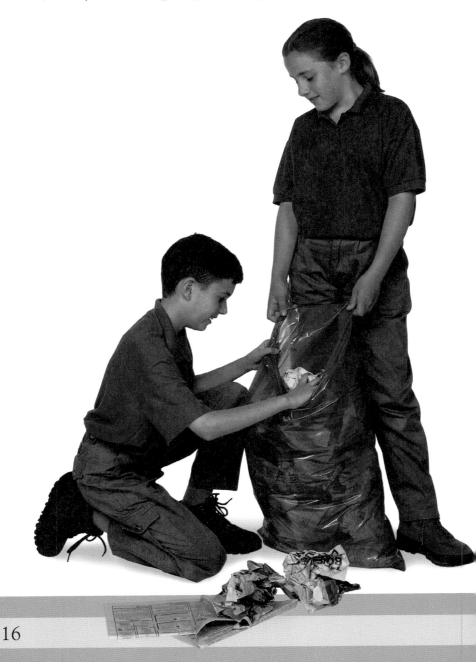

Getting rid of all the trash we make is hard. Making less trash is the first step. Less trash will mean less pollution.

Another way to help make less pollution is to reuse things many times. Instead of using a new lunch bag every day, we could use the same lunch box many times. This makes less trash.

To **recycle** means to change something so it can be used again. We make less trash when we recycle. Lots of things can be recycled. Can you think of things to recycle?

# Protecting Plants And Animals

Earth changes all the time. Forests change. Sometimes people cause forests to change. Forests change when people cut down trees.

People do not make all the changes. Fires and storms change forests when they kill trees.

When trees are lost, animals can lose their homes. People can plant new trees. It takes a long time for trees to grow big. Even so, it is important to plant new trees. This helps the living things of the forest.

Sometimes people make changes to the Earth that hurt living things. Animals and plants lose their homes when people build where they live.

A refuge is a place where animals and plants can be safe. People are not allowed to live in refuges. People can protect living things by creating refuges.

Earth is full of natural resources. We need to protect them and use them with care. What can you do to help?

# Glossary

| | |
|---|---|
| **boulder** | a very large rock |
| **erosion** | when rocks or soil are moved by water or wind |
| **minerals** | nonliving materials that come from the Earth |
| **natural resource** | a useful thing that comes from nature |
| **pollution** | when something harmful is added to the land, air, or water |
| **recycle** | to change something so it can be used again |
| **sand** | tiny pieces of rock |
| **weathering** | the breaking apart and changing of rocks by ice, wind, and rain |